layTime® Piano

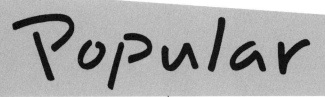

Popular

10 EDITION

Level 1

5-Finger Melodies

This book belongs to:  srisha.V

Arranged by

Nancy and Randall Faber

Production Coordinator: Jon Ophoff
Design and Illustration: Terpstra Design, San Francisco
Engraving: Dovetree Productions, Inc.

FABER
PIANO ADVENTURES®
3042 Creek Drive
Ann Arbor, Michigan 48108

P9-DNT-689

A NOTE TO TEACHERS

PlayTime® Piano Popular offers an exciting set of popular arrangements for the beginning piano student. The selections have been carefully chosen for their special appeal.

These 5-finger melodies reinforce note reading using popular sounds that delight young ears and inspire practicing.

PlayTime® Piano Popular is part of the *PlayTime® Piano* series. "PlayTime" designates Level 1 of the *PreTime® to BigTime® Piano Supplementary Library* arranged by Faber and Faber.

Following are the levels of the supplementary library, which lead from *PreTime®* to *BigTime®*.

PreTime® Piano	(Primer Level)
PlayTime® Piano	(Level 1)
ShowTime® Piano	(Level 2A)
ChordTime® Piano	(Level 2B)
FunTime® Piano	(Level 3A-3B)
BigTime® Piano	(Level 4-above)

Each level offers books in a variety of styles, making it possible for the teacher to offer stimulating material for every student. For a complimentary detailed listing, e-mail faber@pianoadventures.com or write us at the mailing address below.

Visit **www.PianoAdventures.com**.

Teacher Duets

Optional teacher duets are a valuable feature of the *PlayTime® Piano* series. Although the arrangements stand complete on their own, the duets provide a fullness of harmony and rhythmic vitality. And not incidentally, they offer the opportunity for parent and student to play together.

Helpful Hints:

1. The student should know his or her part thoroughly before the teacher duet is used. Accurate rhythm is especially important.

2. Rehearsal numbers are provided to give the student and teacher starting places.

3. The teacher may wish to count softly a measure aloud before beginning, as this will help the ensemble.

ISBN 978-1-61677-001-3

TABLE OF CONTENTS

Hand Placement

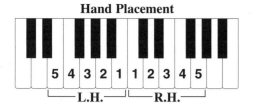

This Land Is Your Land

Words and Music by
WOODY GUTHRIE

Lively

This land is your land, (rest!) this land is my land,

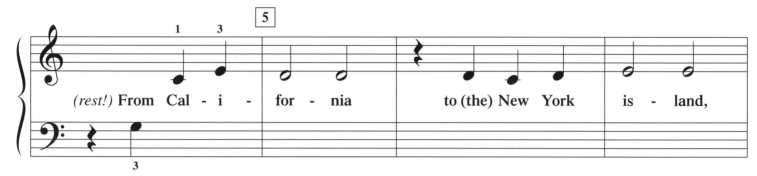

(rest!) From Cal - i - for - nia to (the) New York is - land,

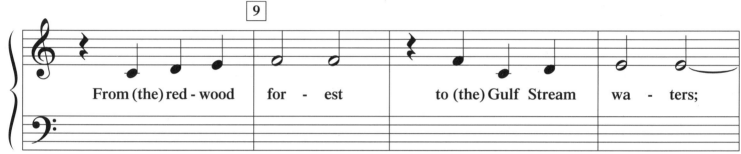

From (the) red - wood for - est to (the) Gulf Stream wa - ters;

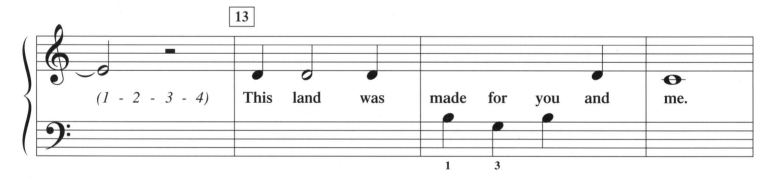

(1 - 2 - 3 - 4) This land was made for you and me.

Teacher Duet: (Student plays 1 octave higher)

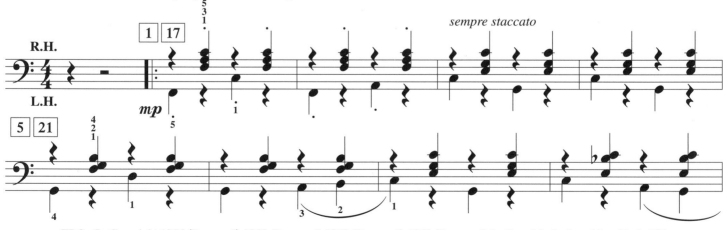

sempre staccato

FF1001

As I was walk - ing that ribbon of high - way,
I saw a - bove me that end - less sky - way;
I saw be - low me that gold - en val - ley;
(1 - 2 - 3 - 4) This land was made for you and me.

ABC

Words and Music by ALPHONSO MIZELL,
FREDERICK PERREN, DEKE RICHARDS, and BERRY GORDY

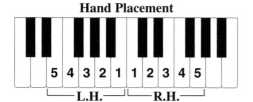

With energy

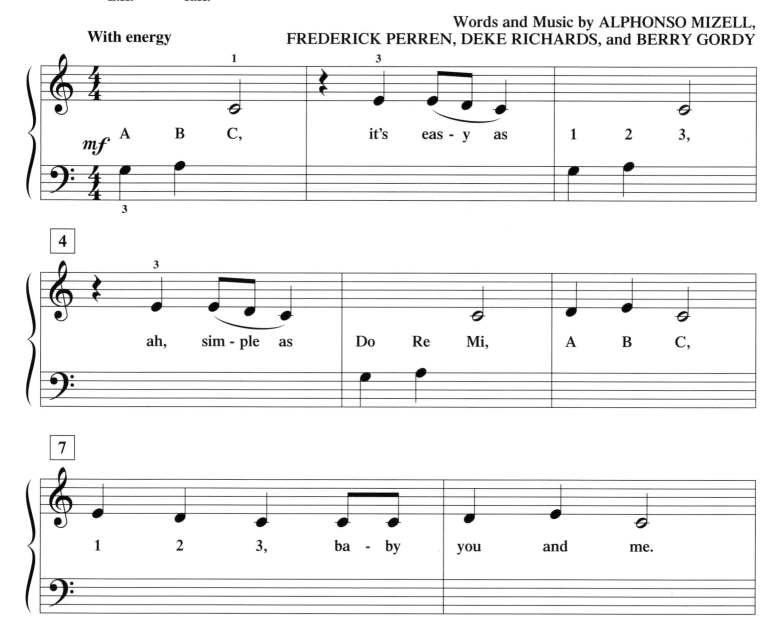

A B C, it's eas-y as 1 2 3,

ah, sim-ple as Do Re Mi, A B C,

1 2 3, ba-by you and me.

Teacher Duet: (Student plays 1 octave higher)

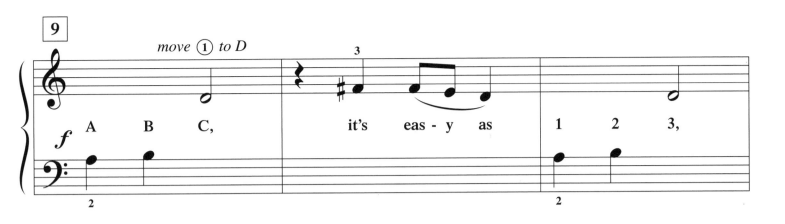

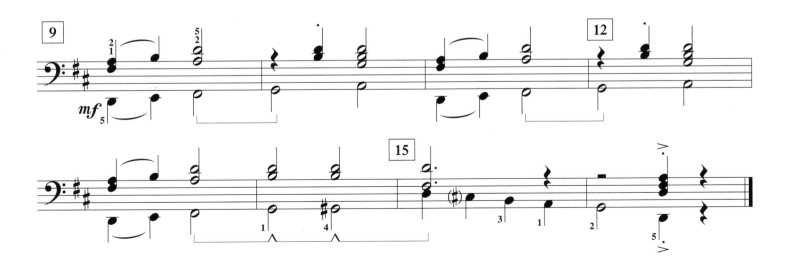

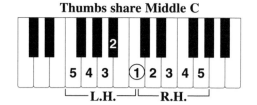

Take Me Out to the Ball Game

Music by ALBERT VON TILZER
Words by JACK NORWORTH

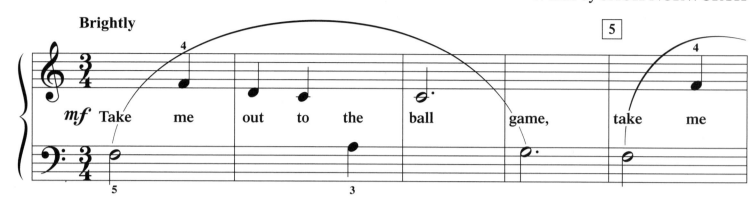

Take me out to the ball game, take me

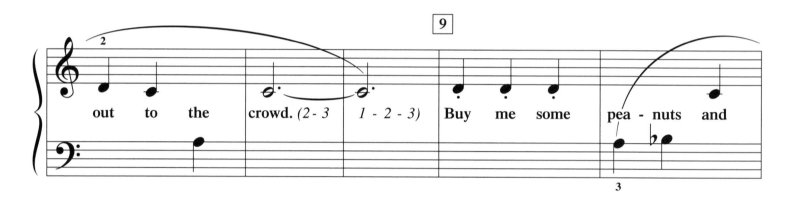

out to the crowd. *(2 - 3   1 - 2 - 3)* Buy me some pea - nuts and

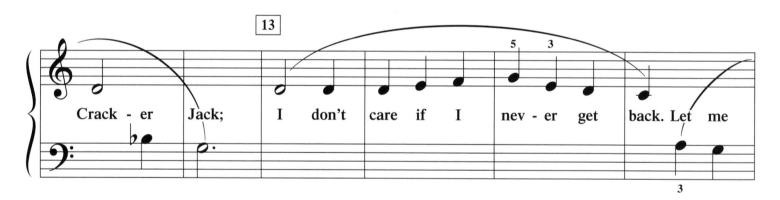

Crack - er Jack; I don't care if I nev - er get back. Let me

Teacher Duet: (Student plays 1 octave higher)

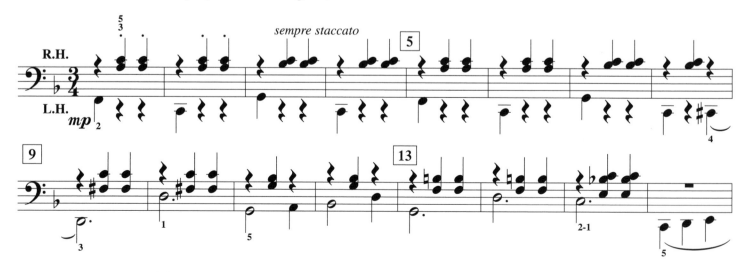

from the movies
Star Wars and *The Empire Strikes Back*

Star Wars (Main Theme)

Music by
JOHN WILLIAMS

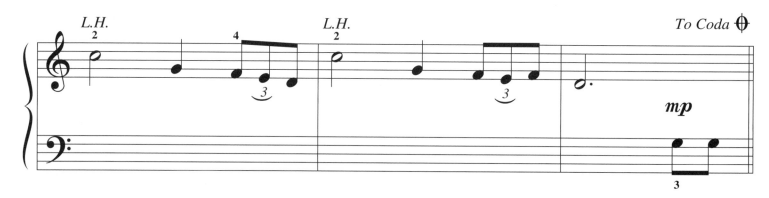

Teacher Duet: (Student plays 1 octave higher)

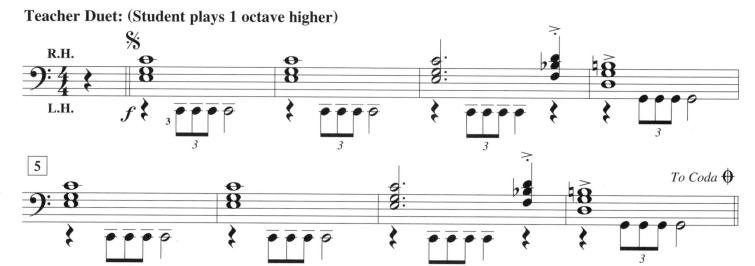

12

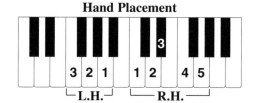

Rocky Top

BOUDLEAUX BRYANT and FELICE BRYANT

Brightly

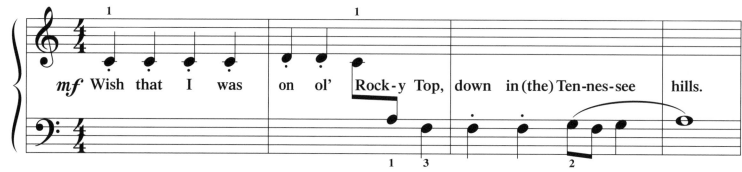

Wish that I was on ol' Rock-y Top, down in (the) Ten-nes-see hills.

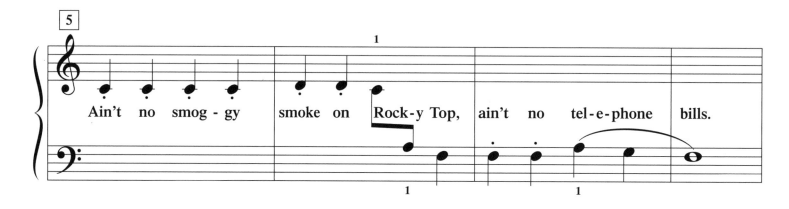

Ain't no smog-gy smoke on Rock-y Top, ain't no tel-e-phone bills.

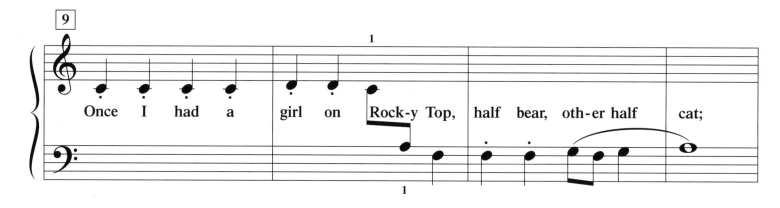

Once I had a girl on Rock-y Top, half bear, oth-er half cat;

Teacher Duet: (Student plays 1 octave higher)

sempre staccato

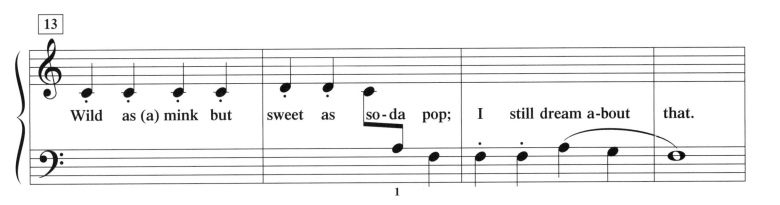

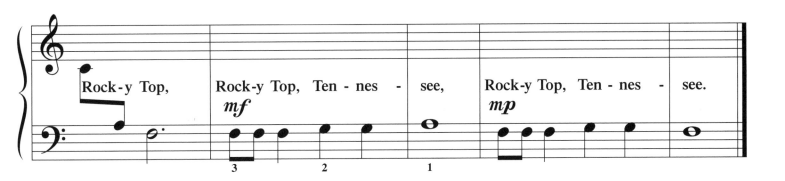

from Walt Disney's *Mary Poppins*

Supercalifragilisticexpialidocious

Words and Music by
RICHARD M. SHERMAN and **ROBERT B. SHERMAN**

Fast and peppy

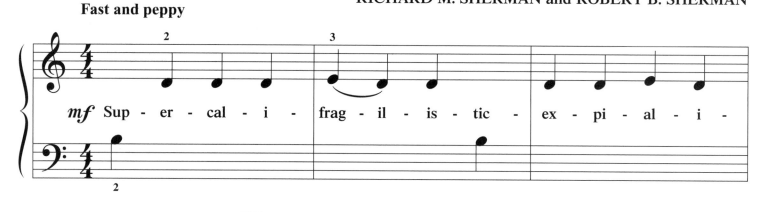

Sup - er - cal - i - frag - il - is - tic - ex - pi - al - i -

do - cious! E - ven though the sound of it is

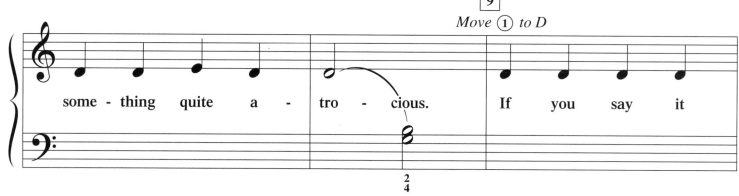

Move ① to D

some - thing quite a - tro - cious. If you say it

Teacher Duet: (Student plays 1 octave higher)

sempre staccato

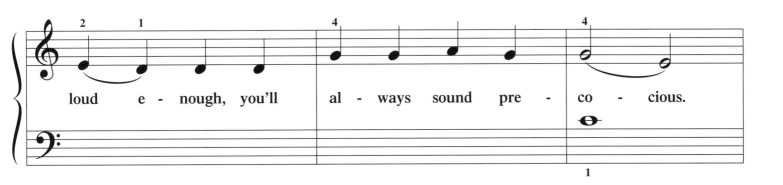

loud   e - nough, you'll | al - ways   sound   pre - co - cious.

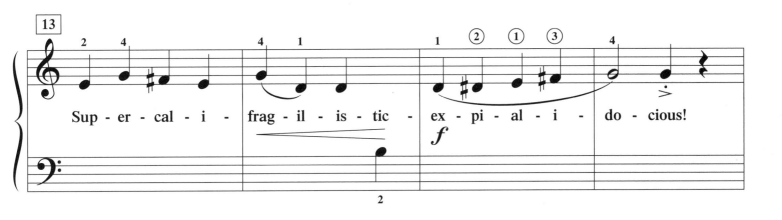

13
Sup - er - cal - i - frag - il - is - tic - ex - pi - al - i - do - cious!

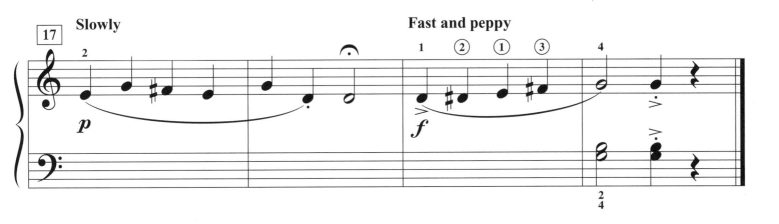

17 Slowly   **Fast and peppy**

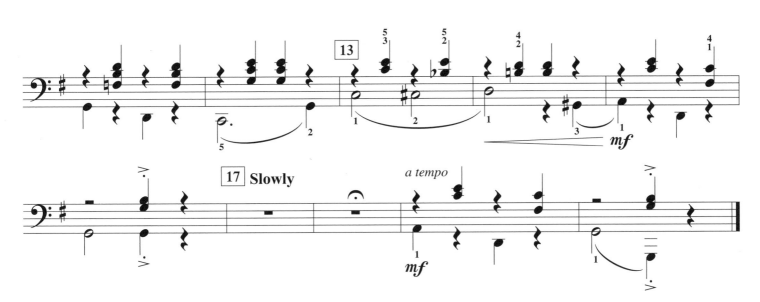

Hand Placement

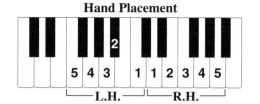

(Meet) The Flintstones

WILLIAM HANNA, JOSEPH BARBERA,
and HOYT S. CURTIN

Fast and fun

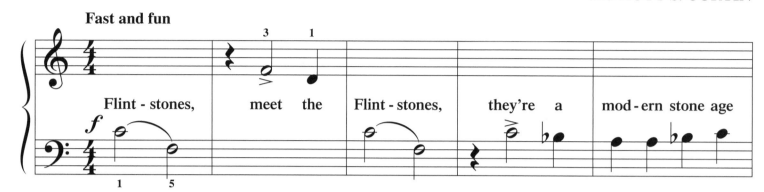

Flint - stones, meet the Flint - stones, they're a mod - ern stone age

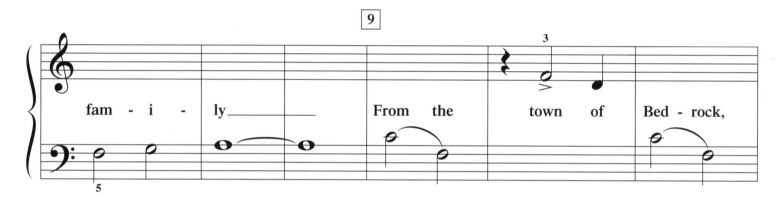

fam - i - ly_____ From the town of Bed - rock,

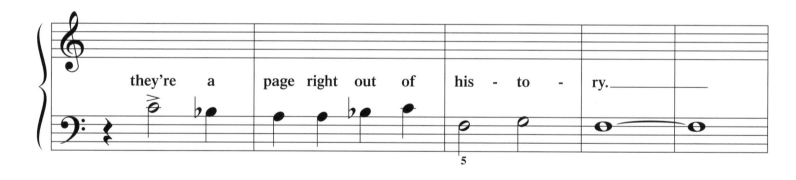

they're a page right out of his - to - ry._____

Teacher Duet: (Student plays 1 octave higher)

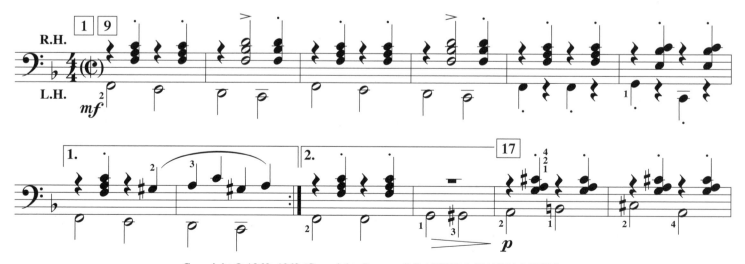

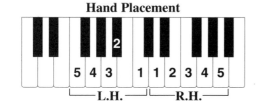

Puff, the Magic Dragon

Words and Music by
PETER YARROW and LEONARD LIPTON

Moderately fast

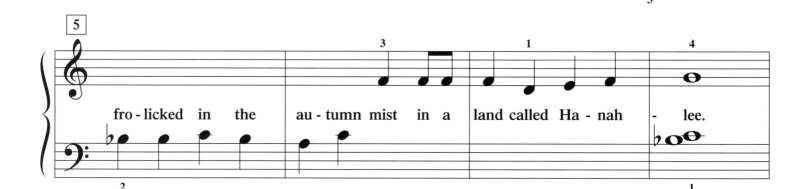

mp Puff, the mag - ic drag - on lived by the sea and

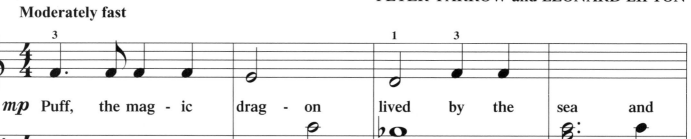

fro - licked in the au - tumn mist in a land called Ha - nah - lee.

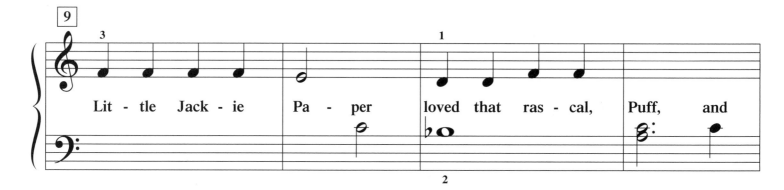

Lit - tle Jack - ie Pa - per loved that ras - cal, Puff, and

Teacher Duet: (Student plays 1 octave higher)

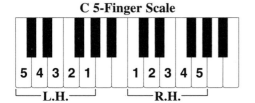

C 5-Finger Scale

Music Box Dancer

Music by
FRANK MILLS

Rather fast

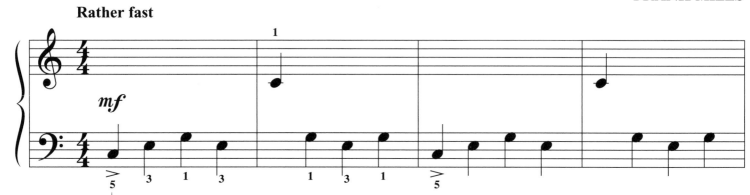

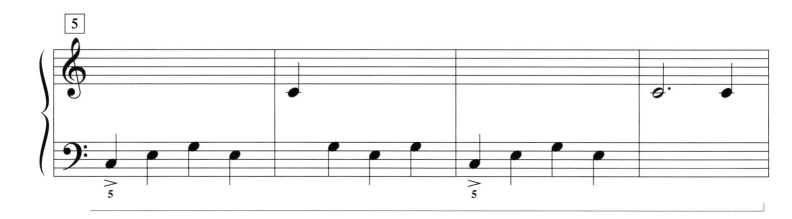

Jump 5 to C!

Teacher Duet: (Student plays 2 octaves higher without pedal)

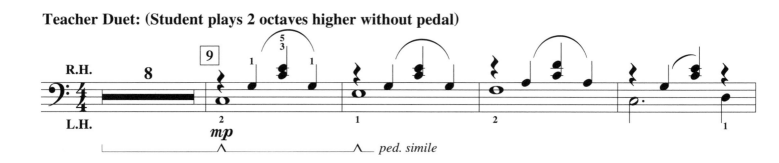

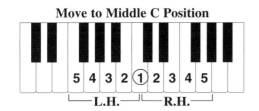

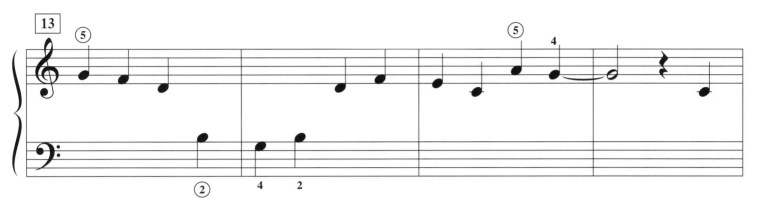

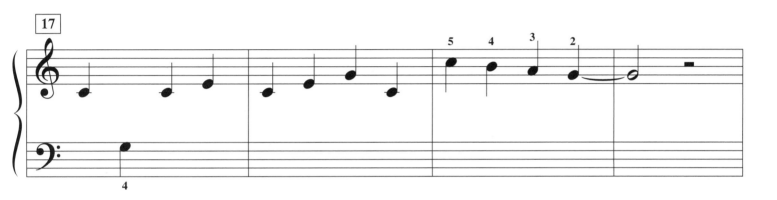

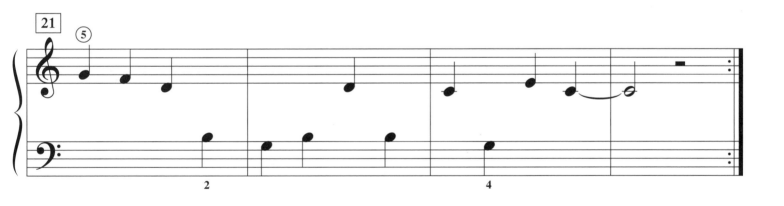

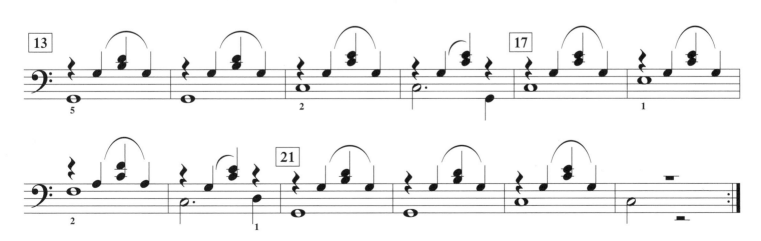

from *The Sound of Music*

Do-Re-Mi

Lyrics by OSCAR HAMMERSTEIN II
Music by RICHARD RODGERS

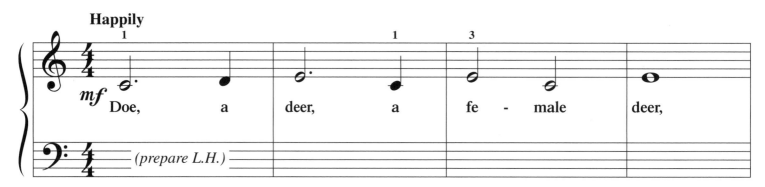

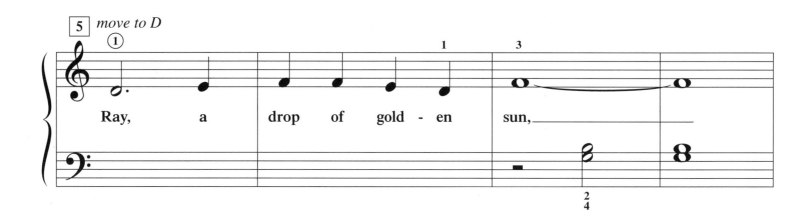

Teacher Duet: (Student plays 1 octave higher)

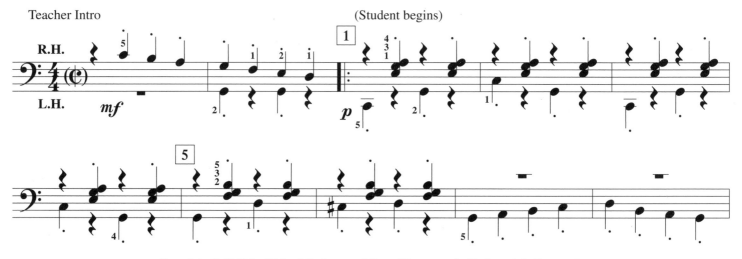

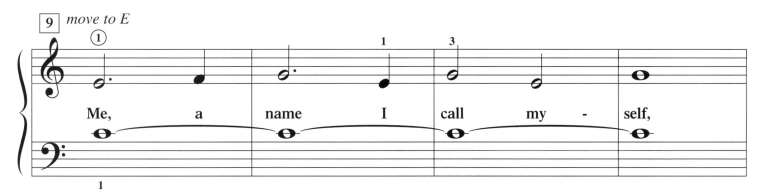

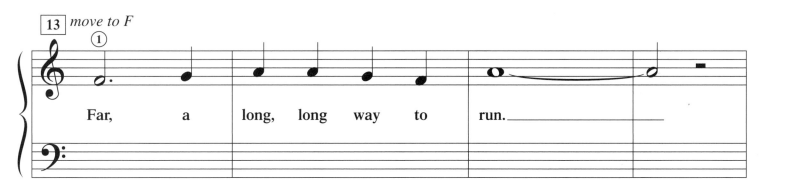

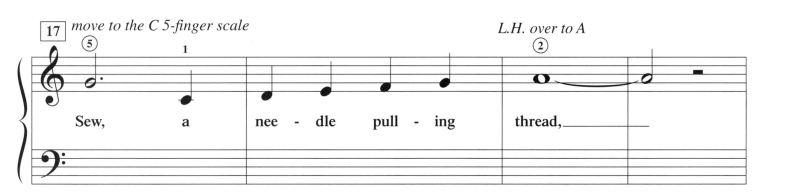

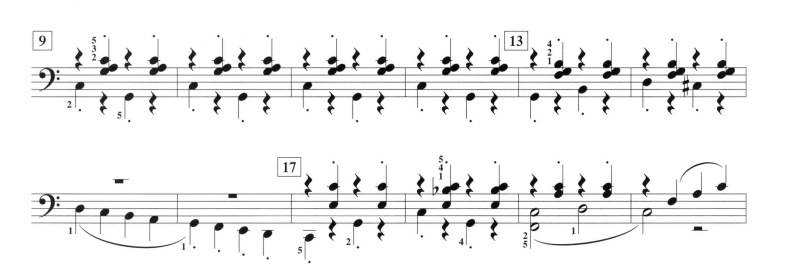